The Holy Spirit in Me

Carolyn Nystrom

ILLUSTRATED BY EIRA B. REEVES

Text © 1981 by The Moody Bible
Institute of Chicago
Design © 1993 Tim Dowley & Peter
Wyart trading as Three's Company

First published in this edition by
Moody Press in 1993
5th printing 1999

ISBN: 0–8024–7858–1

Designed and created by
Three's Company, 5 Dryden Street,
London WC2E 9NW
Worldwide co-edition organized and
produced by Angus Hudson Ltd,
Concorde House, Grenville Place,
London NW7 3SA
fax +44 181 959 3678

Printed in Singapore

Moody Press, a ministry of the Moody
Bible Institute, is designed for
education, evangelization, and
edification. If we may assist you in
knowing more about Christ and the
Christian life, please write us without
obligation: Moody Press, c/o MLM,
Chicago, Illinois, 60610.

Do you know the Holy Spirit? I do.
He lives in me. Let me tell you about Him.

Long ago, before there was a world, God began to create. He formed the earth, a shapeless mass of muck—cold and empty and dark. But God's Spirit was moving over the waters. Soon everything in the world began to take a beautiful form. That's the way the Holy Spirit works.

2 Peter 1:20–21

After God made the world, He created people. Soon more and more people filled the earth. Fathers told their children about God, but sometimes the stories got mixed up. And some people never heard of God at all. God wanted everyone to know Him, so the Holy Spirit showed certain people what to write in a book about God.

4

That book is the Bible. The Bible is God speaking to us.

Long after God made the world, Jesus came to earth. Just before Jesus began to teach, the Holy Spirit came down from heaven to stay with Jesus. Then God's voice sounded from heaven and said, "This is My Son; I am pleased with Him."

Ever since that time, the Holy Spirit has helped people to know Jesus.

John 16:7–11; Romans 8:14–17

Before I knew Jesus, I worried about bad things I'd done. But then I discovered that Jesus would forgive all of those sins—take them away forever. It was the Holy Spirit who helped me see what I had done wrong.

Even now, whenever I begin to wonder if I really do belong in God's family, the Holy Spirit helps me believe.

John 14:16–18

When Jesus was about to leave earth and go back to His Father in heaven, His friends felt sad. They knew they would be lonely. But Jesus promised that the Holy Spirit would take His place on earth. "The Holy Spirit is *with* you, and soon He will be *in* you," Jesus said. "I will never leave you alone."

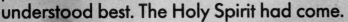

After Jesus had gone back to heaven, His friends waited together for the Holy Spirit to come to them. But they didn't know exactly what would happen. Suddenly a rushing wind filled the house. Tiny flames of fire rested on each person, but no one was hurt. Instead they all began to speak in strange languages.

What do you think they talked about? You guessed it: Jesus. Each person who stood outside the house heard about Jesus in the words he understood best. The Holy Spirit had come.

Romans 12:4–8; 1 Corinthians 12:4–11; 12:27–31; Ephesians 4:11

Along with the ability to speak in other languages, the Holy Spirit brought many other gifts to the friends of Jesus. These were not presents that they could see and touch, but special power to do God's work.

speak God's message

help people work together

serve

encourage others

heal the sick

share

teach

work miracles

faith

speak with unknown languages

bring people into God's family

knowledge

wisdom

kindness

lead others

help anyone who needs help

apostles

know when the Holy Spirit is working

pastors

11

1 Corinthians 12:12–26

The Holy Spirit gave different gifts to each person because God planned for each one to do his own special job. But all the gifts helped Jesus' friends take care of each other. And together they worked for God.

Acts 3:1–10

Using the gift of healing, Peter and John made a man, too sick to walk, well enough to run and jump.

1 Timothy 4:6

Using the gift of pastor, Timothy worked as leader of a new church.

Acts 16:14–15, 40

Using the gift of helps, Lydia invited Paul and his friends to stay in her home while he preached to the people of her city.

Acts 4:23–31

Using the gift of faith, a large group prayed that they would be brave enough to tell others about Jesus even if soldiers put their leaders in jail. And God made them so brave that hundreds more believed.

Ever since the day the Holy Spirit filled that room where people waited, He lives inside each person who believes in Jesus. He is God living in me. He will never leave me, and I will never leave Him.

The Bible says that our bodies are the temple of the Holy Spirit. I want my body to be a good place for God to live. So I eat the right foods. (I don't like green vegetables, but I eat them anyway.) I sleep enough to feel rested. (Sometimes that means I have to go to bed earlier than I really want to.) And I see my doctor when I'm sick. I do all that to keep my body healthy—for God.

Romans 8:8–11

Because the Holy Spirit is in me, He goes where I go: to school, to church, to play with my friends. He is with me at night when I wake up from a scary dream. And He helps me feel quiet and sleepy again.

I remember that when I gave myself to Jesus,
Jesus gave me the Holy Spirit. And I thank
Jesus.

Because the Holy Spirit goes everywhere with me, He goes some places that God would not want to go. The Holy Spirit was there the day I pulled Linda off the swing. The Holy Spirit was there when I sat behind our house and practiced saying bad words. The Holy Spirit was there the night I said, "I don't want to pray," and turned over and went to sleep.

The Bible says, "Don't make the Holy Spirit sad."

I try not to do things that make the Holy Spirit sad, but I do not have to try all by myself. The Holy Spirit helps me say no to sin.

Just yesterday, when I was playing at Linda's house, I saw a necklace on her dresser. I wanted that necklace so much that I almost put it in my pocket. But I didn't. The Holy Spirit helped me not to steal.

The Holy Spirit helps in other ways. The Holy Spirit helps me to learn about Jesus. Sometimes He helps my Sunday school teacher tell my class an interesting Bible story. Sometimes He helps Mom answer my questions about God. Sometimes He just helps my mind understand what is hard even for grown-ups. And after that, the Holy Spirit helps me remember it all.

I will never leave you

The Holy Spirit helps me tell others about Jesus. God wants many people in His family, and He wants me to show them how to come to Him. The Holy Spirit helps me say just the right words that would bring them to Jesus.

23

Acts 16:6–10

The Holy Spirit helps me to make good choices—even without my knowing it. Like the time I chose to ride my bike to the pond instead of to the woods. Later I found out that a swarm of bees had landed in the woods that day.

Ephesians 4:4–6

The Holy Spirit helps me to love other people in God's family. There's Granny Tucker, who is eighty years old and needs a wheelchair at

TO THE
POND

church, and Janey Skaggs, who is sixteen and goes shopping with me, and Priscilla Watts, who doesn't have any family near here, but she always has Sunday dinner with us. We are in God's family together, so the Holy Spirit helps us to love each other.

Romans 8:26–27

And the Holy Spirit helps me pray. If I don't know how to pray, the Holy Spirit teaches me. Even if I don't know what to ask God for, the Holy Spirit prays for me. And God understands.

John 14:16

When you think of all those different jobs, what do you think might be another name for the Holy Spirit? That's right. The Bible calls Him the "Helper."

The Bible says that people who belong to God are like trees. (Of course we don't look like trees. The Bible is speaking of what we do, not the way we look.) The tree behind my house gives us apples every fall. It is an apple tree, so apples are its fruit.

Just so, the Holy Spirit in us causes us to give the fruit of the Spirit.

kindness

patience

self-control

joy

love

goodness

gentleness

peace

faithfulness

29

When I help my friends stop fighting, when I am patient about a broken shoestring, when I am gentle with my kitten, then I am giving out the fruit of the Spirit. And I am happy. So is the Spirit in me.